UITGAVEN VAN HET
NEDERLANDS HISTORISCH-ARCHAEOLOGISCH INSTITUUT TE İSTANBUL

Publications de l'Institut historique et archéologique néerlandais de Stamboul

sous la direction de
A. A. CENSE et A. A. KAMPMAN

IV

THE ARCHAEOLOGICAL MUSEUM OF THE
AMERICAN UNIVERSITY OF BEIRUT

THE ARCHAEOLOGICAL MUSEUM OF THE
AMERICAN UNIVERSITY OF BEIRUT

BY

D. C. BARAMKI

Professor of Archaeology at the American University of Beirut

İSTANBUL
NEDERLANDS HISTORISCH-ARCHAEOLOGISCH INSTITUUT
IN HET NABIJE OOSTEN
1959

PLATES

I. 1. Juglet of Copper Age from Byblos.
    2. Small jar of the Copper Age from Palestine.
    3. Painted piriform juglet of the Middle Bronze Age from Syria.
    4. Trumpet based bowl of the Middle Bronze Age from Palestine.

II. 5. Bronze toggle pins of the Middle and Late Bronze Ages from Phoenicia.
    6 & 7. Bronze figurine of Reshef from the Late Bronze Age from Phoenicia.

III. 8. Decanter of the Late Bronze Age from Phoenicia.
     9. Mycenaean stirrup vase of the Late Bronze Age from Phoenicia.
    10. Beer jug of the Early Iron Age with strainer spout from Phoenicia.
    11. Beer jug of the Iron Age from Phoenicia.

IV. 12. Painted juglet of the Iron Age from Phoenicia.
    13. Small juglet of the Iron Age from Phoenicia.
    14. Decanter of the Middle Iron Age from Palestine.
    15. Slender jar of the Persian Period from Phoenicia.

V. 16. Hellenistic storage jar from Phoenicia.
    17. Hellenistic jar from Phoenicia.
    18. Moulded glass bowl of the Iron Age from Phoenicia.
    19. Glass bowl of the Roman Period from Phoenicia.

VI. 20. Glass vase of the Roman Period from Phoenicia.
    21. Terra cotta figurine of the Roman Period from Phoenicia.
    22. Bronze figurine of Venus of the Roman Period from Phoenicia.
    23. Palmyrene bust of the Third Century AD.

THE ARCHAEOLOGICAL MUSEUM OF THE
AMERICAN UNIVERSITY OF BEIRUT [1])

One of the important educational services which the founders of the American University of Beirut rendered to the Near East was the establishment of an archaeological Museum in Beirut, at a time when the entire area boasted of only two museums, one in Cairo and the other at Constantinople. By embarking on this measure, the University has saved for the Near East many a valuable ancient artefact which would otherwise have probably found its way into some private collection and possible oblivion, and also, it has helped to inculcate in the inhabitants of the area a deep appreciation of the heritage of the glorious past of the Near East.

Since the foundation of the Museum at the University in 1868 many other museums have been established in the Near East, namely, at Beirut, Baghdad, Mosul, Jerusalem, Amman, Damascus, Aleppo and elsewhere. These Museums quite rightly contain the very important artefacts and the great works of art of the past discovered in the area which no student of archaeology can afford to ignore, and a visit to any one of these museums affords a rich and useful experience to the visitor. Although the Museum of the University does not boast of such great works of art as any of these national museums yet it still renders a great service to the area as a whole; each of the Museums cited is strictly local, and its main purpose is to present the cultural progress of the country in which it is situated; this it must be admitted has been done admirably in all the Museums in question. The role of the Museum of the University has taken a new turn. Its collection embraces artefacts from all sections of the Near East, from Iraq, Iran, Syria, Phoenicia, Cyprus, Egypt and Palestine. For a comparative study of the ancient cultures of the countries of the Near East it is perhaps unequalled and indispensable.

The founders of the American University of Beirut, or Syrian Protestant College as it was then called, therefore showed great foresight in establishing

---

[1]) This survey appeared in *Al Kulliyah* in two parts under the title *A Journey Back through Time*. It is reprinted here with some modifications, at the request of the editors of this series.

a Museum soon after the foundation of the institution. From a modest beginning formed around a nucleus presented by General Cesnola, the American
Consul in Cyprus in the middle of the last century, the collection has grown
by slow degrees into a large Museum where a visitor can get a cross section
of the cultural progress of man in the entire area of the Near East from the
Early Stone Age down to relatively recent times. The value of the collection
both to students and to the general public is great.

The story of the growth of the collection is closely linked with the gradual
expansion of the parent institution, the University. The Museum grew mainly
by purchase from the meagre funds which the University, despite its heavy
commitments in other essential services, was able to allocate to the Museum
from time to time, and also from a number of gifts donated by the Alumni
and friends of the University, such as the collection of classical sculpture
which was presented by the late Dr. H. H. Jessup, the group of Graeco-Roman
inscriptions which were donated by Mr. Baroody, some pottery from Palestine
which was given by Dr. Frederic J. Bliss, a number of inscribed fragments of
Egyptian alabaster vases which were presented by Mr. V. E. Macy and the
large collection of the late Dr. Dorman which was presented to the Museum
by Mrs. Dorman. The available funds placed at the disposal of the successive
curators of the Museum have enabled them to add to the collection by slow
degrees that over a great number of years the University has become the
proud possessor of over 9000 well selected artefacts of various types, and a
very valuable and rich collection of coins over 10,000 in number, besides
numerous duplicates which can be used in exchange with other similar
institutions.

Credit for this achievement must in a large measure go to Professor George
E. Post, Professor of Botany and Surgery, who took charge of the Museum
in addition to his other duties. In 1899 Dr. Post successfully launched a fund
raising campaign for a science building, with a substantial initial contribution
from Mr. Morris Jessup. Dr. Post personally designed and supervized the
construction of the new building which was completed in 1902. In recognition
of his untiring efforts, the new building was called after him, and the University Museum came to occupy a major part in it. Just as great a debt is due to
to Dr. Harvey Porter, who soon after his arrival in 1870, collaborated with
Dr. Post in the administration of the Museum. Under his charge the growth
of the Museum was greatly accelerated by the purchase of fairly substantial
private collections from individuals living in the Near East. In 1904, Dr.
Porter acquired a collection of Palmyrene busts, following this up in the
ensuing year by the acquisition of the Rouvier collection of ancient artefacts

from Egypt, Cyprus, Athens and North Africa, as well as part of his important collection of Graeco-Roman coins of the Near East. Two years later, in 1907 Dr. Porter acquired Mr. Merrill's important collection of Palestinian antiquities. Mr. Merrill was the American Consul in Jerusalem for a number of years before the First World War, just about the time when interest in Palestinian archaeology was at its height, and when a number of foreign institutions had expeditions working in the field.

Dr. Porter remained the Curator of the Museum even after his retirement from teaching at the University. In the early twenties he engaged Mr. (now Sir Leonard) Woolley to classify the collection and write a short Guide to the Museum of Archaeology. Dr. Porter was succeeded by Professor Nelson first as Professor of History and eventually as Curator of the Museum. His deep knowledge of hieroglyphics soon took him to Egypt, to the great loss of the University. However, during the short time that he held charge of the Museum, he was able to read and translate the hieroglyphic inscriptions in the Museum. The Museum was next placed in charge of Professor Alfred E. Day, who because of his interest in the Stone Age, greatly augmented the flint collection in the Museum.

In 1931 through the generosity of a Lebanese American woman resident in New York, a chair in Archaeology was established at the American University of Beirut. The first holder was Dr. Harald Ingholt who had earlier been excavating tombs at Palmyra. Dr. Ingholt founded "Berytus" a periodical dealing with archaeological studies, and added the Ford Collection of small antiquities to the University Museum.

Owing to adverse trade conditions, the chair in Archaeology lapsed at the American University of Beirut, and there being no funds for the engagement of a curator, Mrs. Dodge kindly stepped in and took charge. Mrs. Dodge was faced with the arduous task of packing the large collection and removing it to places of greater safety on account of the approach of the Second World War. The exhibition galleries had to be used as stores of food supplies.
The collection lay dormant until the end of 1947 when through the generosity of a friend of the American University of Beirut who wishes to remain anonymous, a new Curator, the late Mrs. Dorothy Mackay, was appointed in January 1948. Mrs. Mackay had to unpack and re-arrange the collection in time for the meeting of UNESCO at Beirut in November of the same year. She performed the task admirably and the Museum was soon restored to its former use, as a kaleidoscope of the material culture of the various ages and areas of the Near East. The present arrangement is substantially her own, but

in view of the great increase in the number of artefacts acquired during the last seven years, some alterations have had to be introduced here and there by the present writer. The Museum is in the happy position now of being able to dispense with purchases of any but the most essential artefacts which have an educational value and merit, or which form valuable groups of finds from known localities.

A Museum of Archaeology, however, cannot remain static if it is to maintain its use as a laboratory for the cultural study of the past. However, as growth by purchase, except in exceptional circumstances, is to be deprecated, the Museum can and must only grow from now on by acquisitions from archaeological excavations. It is not always the value of an ancient artefact per se that is of interest to the scientist; but its locus and its context, or in other words its position in a stratified occupational level, are sometimes of far greater importance in the study of the past than the object itself. The University has recently embarked on archaeological excavations, and has happily struck beginners' luck. It is thus anticipated that the Museum will grow more from the ancient artefacts coming from excavations undertaken by the University, rather than from other sources, and the scientific value of the collection will thus be greatly enhanced. Apart from serving the interests of archaeology, the University will from now on be making valuable contributions to the study of the ancient culture of the Near East, and has already made a good start by bringing to light a hitherto unknown culture in its excavations at Tell el Ghassil. Indeed for a proper understanding of the present civilization of any area, a study of its ancient cultural background and heritage is essential, and the Near East is no exception.

At present the collection of antiquities in the University Museum is exhibited in 7 table-cases, 17 wall-cases, 4 iron-bound-cases and 3 bronze cases arranged as far as possible in chronological order. Examples of Graeco-Roman sculpture and other large objects are dispersed around the walls of the Museum as close to their chronological sequence as feasible. It is hoped in the near future to relieve this congestion, and to spread the exhibits over a large number of cases, when the Central Gallery in Post Hall is restored to the Museum.
The first case in the Museum, Case 1, contains artefacts of the Palaeolithic Age, starting with those of the Lower Palaeolithic Age, namely, Abbevillian and Acheulian clumsy handaxes which were used from about 450,000 to 180,000 years ago by an uncertain species of the human race, who used to live on tops of trees and on riverside terraces, using the hand-axe both as a weapon for hunting and as a tool for skinning animals. Next, in the same Case, there is a display of the better shaped Levallois-Mousterian flakes and

cores of the Middle Palaeolithic Age of Neanderthal man (180,000 - 80,000 years ago), who took shelter in caves on account of the approaching Fourth Ice Age. These are followed by the more useful and handy flint points, borers, gravers and scrapers of the Upper Palaeolithic Age (80,000 - 10,000 years ago) of homo sapiens; the latter collection comes mainly from the excavations of Ksar 'Akil near Antelyas, and represents no less than six phases starting about 80,000 years ago and ending about 10,000 years ago. In the last stage of the Palaeolithic Age man continued to live in caves, but he hunted in groups with long range weapons, such as flint-headed arrows, and used more specialized tools, of which some are displayed in the case in question.

The next case, Case 2, is reserved for the Mesolithic and Neolithic Ages. Microlithic flint implements used by man during the Mesolithic or Middle Stone Age (8000-5500 BC.) are displayed together with a number of sickle-blades. This age witnessed the introduction of agriculture on a very modest scale, but from the small beginning made in this period great changes in the economy of the human race were to follow in the ensuing Neolithic or New Stone Age (5500-4000 BC.).

The Neolithic Age brought with it changes of a revolutionary nature in human culture. The value of agriculture having been tested, and its value realized, it was soon adopted as the principal source of man's sustenance. The small patch of ground outside the cave, which was found adequate during the Mesolithic Age, proved insufficient for Neolithic man; he, perhaps Natufian man, descended from his caves up in the hills to settle down in the plains and cultivate a more extensive area. To protect his crops he had to live near his fields, and this led to the second momentous change or innovation, namely the introduction of construction and architecture into world history. Man's new complicated life required more vessels to store his goods; the animal skins of his predecessors were inadequate for a settled way of life; to meet this new challenge he proceeded to carve vessels out of stone, and followed this up by inventing pottery vessels.

These great changes are reflected in the exhibits in Case 2, where there is a display of a large number of axe-heads, tied to hafts, which Neolithic man used for felling trees with which to roof his huts, hoes which were used to till the ground, serpentine celts which were used both as weapons and amulets, as well as arrow-heads, lance-heads, knives, saws and awls, all except the celts being made of flint. But besides flint tools, Neolithic man had bone implements, such as needles, pins, handles for implements and so on. These were sharpened on pebble hones picked up in river beds. In the same case there are a few examples of Neolithic pottery decorated with deeply incised lines.

Through a generous exchange with the Department of Antiquities in Iraq, the Museum has recently acquired a large number of objects, mostly pottery, from the Neolithic and Chalcolithic Ages of Mesopotamia. These are at present exhibited in Case 3, and include flints from Jarmo (c. 5000 - 4800 BC.), pottery from Hassuna (4800 - 4600 BC.) including fragments of a husking tray, incised ware, incised and painted ware, and painted ware, covering all stages of the culture of the site; painted pottery from Samarra (4600 - 4300 BC.); painted pottery from the Halafian Period (4300 - 4000 BC.) also found at Hassuna; Ubeidian painted pottery (4000 - 3500 BC.) from Tell el-Ubeid and Eridu including a necklace made of terra cotta beads; Urukian (3500 - 3200 BC.) burnished pottery from Warka, and painted Jamdat Nasr (3200 - 3000 BC.) pottery from Warka and Uqeir. The case thus conveys at a glimpse the development of the ceramic industry in ancient Iraq from the beginning of the Fifth Millennium to the end of the Fourth.

The large pottery collection in the Museum is displayed in Cases 5-15, 18, 20, 22 and 23, arranged in chronological order, and will be discussed in due course. However it is well to emphasize at this stage the great revolution in man's economy which took place as a result of the discovery of metal. Some metal objects started making their appearance as early as the middle of the Fourth Millennium BC., but these objects were few and far between. As from the beginning of the Third Millennium, greater use was made of copper, and a larger number of tools came to be made from this medium. In Iraq, which maintained the lead in ancient civilizations all through the pre-historic period, there are no metals at all; but when Iraq proceeded in the Fourth Millennium to produce more agricultural products than the population of the country needed, they looked around to see where they could barter their surplus food products for other materials in which the country was deficient. They soon hit upon Magan (modern Oman) as their best source of supply for metal, and entered into trade relations with that country. They imported copper and bronze from Magan and gave some of their surplus agricultural products in exchange. By the beginning of the Third Millennium, the trade in metal had expanded to such an extent that some of the weapons and tools came to be made of copper. At first only daggers and axe-heads were made of this material, but by slow degrees spear-heads, arrow-heads, knives, swords and even scythes came to be made of copper or of bronze. Besides copper, gold and silver were also imported from other regions by barter.

The finds in the so-called "Royal Cemetery at Ur," which belongs to the first half of the Third Millennium, indicate widespread trading activities between Iraq and Arabia, Iran, Asia Minor and Armenia.

The chief users of metal were the cities that rose over the ruins of Chalcolithic villages in the Valleys of the Nile and the Tigris and Euphrates, but as these fall in areas where metal ore was either scarce or unknown, they had to import the ores from the backward hill tribes situated on the periphery of the Fertile Crescent.

The introduction of metal brought with it specialization in industry among the citizens. Thus the population had to divide itself into groups, each group practising its calling and sometimes forming a guild. Apart from raw materials which in many cases were obtained by exchange with finished fancy articles and agricultural products, each city was self sufficient. It had its own building industry, carpenters' workshops, potters, metal-workers, jewellers who made trinkets in gold, silver, bronze and faience, shoe-makers, tailors and above all priests who stepped in to organize the growing community and to rule and direct it.

The potter's art made great advances all over the Near East during the Copper or Early Bronze Age. In Phoenicia some of the better pots were made on a slow moving wheel and burnished over a red slip with a very pleasant diamond pattern (Fig. 1). The commoner type of vessel continued to be made by hand, but great care was taken in the making, showing that the craftsman had real pride in his work. Most of the vessels of the period are provided with cord-eye handles placed at the bottom of the neck, near its juncture with the shoulder of the vessel (Fig. 2).

Sometime in the twenty third dynasty before Christ, the potter's wheel, which was invented much earlier as we saw, came into general use, and about the same time copper was deliberately alloyed with tin to produce bronze; but this was by no means the earliest occasion when bronze was used, because some ore deposits in Magan actually contained natural bronze. Evidence from Byblos, Hama, Jericho and many other sites in Phoenicia, Syria and Palestine shows that the four centuries between the twenty third and the nineteenth century were a period of turmoil and anarchy, due to the weakness of Egypt in the First Intermediate Period and the incursions of the nomads from the desert. It was followed by a period of stability which lasted for three and a half centuries. This period is called the Middle Bronze Age (1900 - 1550 BC.) and represents great progress over the previous period. The products of this age far excel anything that went before or anything that followed it until the Hellenistic Period. In pottery very graceful piriform jars, juglets (Fig. 3) and deep bowls (Fig. 4) were made on the wheel and were sometimes painted with geometric designs in polychrome; bronze toggle pins which were used to

fasten clothes made their appearance; some of these were beautifully orna-
mented with melon heads (Fig. 5).

The last stage of the Bronze Age, the Late Bronze Age, (1550 - 1200 BC.)
showed a falling off in taste, which reflects the uncertainty of the period. It
was the era which witnessed the expulsion of the Hyksos from Egypt, and
the invasion of Canaan by the Egyptian armies under Thothmes III. Yet from
this period comes one of the most important bronze figurines in the Museum
(Fig. 6 & 7). During the last stages of the age, the western horn of the Fertile
Crescent became the scene of the struggle between the Hittites and the
Egyptians, and the two-fold invasion of the Near East by nomadic desert
tribesmen from the East, and by Aegeans from the West. The arrival of the
latter at the beginning of the twelfth century was a turning point in the
history of the Near East. It brought the Bronze Age to a close and ushered
in the Age of Iron. It saw the end of the great Empires and the rise of small
states in Syria, Phoenicia and Palestine.
The ceramic industry of the first two centuries of the Late Bronze Age is a
continuation of the previous age, but burnishing was discarded and replaced
by monochrome painting (Fig. 8). As from the beginning of the Fourteenth
Century a large number of Mycenaean pots were imported from Mycenae
(Fig. 9).

Let us now examine the exhibits in the Museum in relation to the events that
have been discussed. In Case 4, number of alabaster vases of Egyptian manufacture, but actually found at Byblos, bear witness to the trade which
flourished between Egypt and Phoenicia at an early date. The vases belong
to the Old Kingdom and some of them are inscribed with the names of the
Egyptian kings of the Sixth Dynasty. Egypt badly needed timber, and Phoenicia was the closest place where she could get it. Close relations between the
two countries were established as from the beginning of the Third Millennium. The same case contains a number of figurines and toggle-pins in copper,
carnelian, agate and faience beads which were used during the same age, and
an array of bronze weapons which were in use right through the Third and
Second Millennia. A number of mirrors that came into use during the Middle
Bronze Age may be seen in Case 16, while Case 17 tells the story of the
evolution of the lamp from the saucer lamp of the Early Bronze or Copper
Age to the shoe-shaped lamp of the Middle Ages. Egyptian artefacts of the
Chalcolithic Age including Amratian and Gerzean black-topped and painted
pots, one of which is painted with a representation of a Nile boat, are dis-
played in a special iron-bound case, Case A.

In view of the great importance of pottery as an expression of art and also as a criterion for dating, special attention is devoted to it in the University Museum. Pottery of the Chalcolithic Age (4000 - 3000 BC.), Copper Age (3000 - 2300 BC.), the Intermediate Age (2300 - 1900 BC.), the Middle Bronze Age (1900 - 1550 BC.) and the Late Bronze Age (1550 - 1200 BC.) is displayed in four cases, Cases 5-8. Case 5 contains the pottery of these five ages from Palestine. From the Chalcolithic Age, there is a red-slipped cup with an ear handle, similar to another cup discovered by Miss Kenyon in Tomb 94 at Jericho; two juglets with a long spout, and two juglets with large ear-handles. From the pottery of the Copper Age, the Museum has a good selection of wavy ledge handles, one of which has a burnished red slip, small jars with minute cord-eye handles painted in red with a diamond pattern; small jars with cord-eye handles (Fig. 2) some of which are burnished over a red slip and a number of bowls with round bases. Most of the objects from the Copper Age are handmade. From the long Intermediate Period there are a number of caliciform jars of various sizes.

There is a large number of piriform juglets and bowls from the Middle Bronze Age. Most of the juglets have button bases and double strand handles, and all of them have a slip, either red or cream in colour (Fig. 3) The deep bowls sometimes have ogee or trumpet bases, and a cream slip (Fig. 4); some of them are carinated. From the Late Bronze Age, there are a number of deep bowls similar to those of the Middle Bronze Age, but the ogee bases are replaced by disk or flat bases, and the burnishing is not so well done. In addition there are dippers with a more pointed base, and from the second half of the Late Bronze Age the Museum boasts of a number of Cypriote juglets in base-ring ware including some local imitations, and some imitations of Mycenaean lentoid flasks generally called "pilgrim bottles".

The collection of pottery from Phoenicia and Syria of the same five ages, which is exhibited in Case 6, is even richer. There are two juglets of very coarse ware similar to those discovered in the Chalcolithic burials at Byblos, a small bowl with very large grits, and a number of burnished sherds. From the Copper Age, there are a number of pots with cylindrical spouts, pots with flat bases and cord-eye handles similar to those discovered by Guigues at Lebéa, and some figurines of the goddess of fertility. From the Intermediate Period in Syria, there are a number of goblets, painted or ribbed similar to those discovered by Ingholt at Hama, and some pots in burnished black ware which have been turning up in substantial numbers in North Syria. There is a large assortment of piriform juglets of the Middle Bronze Age including juglets painted in polychrome (Fig. 3) from Syria, juglets and dippers with a red burnished slip from Sidon, carinated bowls, and Hyksos black juglets decorated with pin point designs. In addition there are painted jars on tripod stands, decanters painted in polychrome or red slipped and burnished, and examples of black "tea pot ware" similar to those discovered at Megiddo.

Case 7 contains pottery from two Tomb Groups discovered at Byblos. The first tomb was used during both the Copper Age and the Middle Bronze Age. The second belongs entirely to the Middle Bronze Age. In the first tomb, there was a large oval jar with a flat base, with two elliptical handles attached on the opposite sides of the middle of the body; the jar is red slipped, and burnished in a diamond pattern; in addition there is a tall slender juglet and a number of bowls treated in the same way; but the most important vessel in the group is a twin vessel consisting of two attached jars, between which there is a quadruped standing with its forefeet on one vessel, its hind legs on the other, and the head bent over the mouth of one of the vessels as though drinking. All these vessels belong to the Copper Age. In the same tomb, a number of piriform jugs were discovered, decorated on the outside with a comb pattern and a pot painted with a floral pattern in white over a black background. This group belongs to the Middle Bronze Age, and the painted pot no doubt is an importation from Kamares in Crete. The second tomb contained a number of piriform jugs some of which were painted with horizontal bands in red.

Case 8 is reserved for the Late Bronze Age pottery. The first part consists of a number of Mycenaean vessels, including stirrup vases (Fig. 9), lentoid vessels (pilgrim bottles), bowls and dippers, including some local imitations. The rest of the case contains examples of Late Bronze Age pottery which was current in Phoenicia, including some importations from Cyprus and Mycenae. The decanters (Fig. 8) are perhaps worth singling out for special attention. The general characteristics of the ceramic industry of each age is emphasized both in the manner of display, and by means of labels. Thus the ear-handles and gritty ware of the Chalcolithic Age, the cord-eye and ledge-handles of the Early Bronze or Copper Age, the caliciform pots of the Intermediate Age, and the piriform vessels of the Middle Bronze Age are adequately stressed. The Twelfth Century BC. witnessed a great convulsion which shook the ancient world. Three waves of Aegeans who had previously been settled in Greece and on the West Coast of Asia Minor, were driven out of their homes by the onslaught of Dorians and other kindred tribes who had formerly inhabited the Danube Basina. The Aegeans broke lose and set about seeking homes elsewhere. They spread over Asia Minor and the eastern basin of the Mediterranean spreading fire and sword before them. "The Isles are restless disturbed among themselves" wailed the Egyptian chroniclers of the time. The first Aegean wave moved east and destroyed the Hittite Empire in its stride; the second attacked Egypt and although defeated at the Battle of Pelusium, the Aegeans were allowed to settle in South Palestine; they are the Philistines of the Bible. The third wave came down the coast of Phoenicia and destroyed the cities of Alalakh (Tell Atshaneh) near Antioch, Ugarit, modern Ras Shamra near Lattakieh, and Aradus, modern Ruad. Their advent weakened Egypt and so for the first time in history the countries of the Levant were able to enjoy a period of independence.

On the ruins left by the invasion of desert tribes such as the Aramaeans and the Israelites from the east and the onslaught of the Aegeans from the west, several petty kingdoms and principalities arose in Phoenicia, Syria and Palestine. In Phoenicia a large number of maritime city-states arose and established complete control over the Mediterranean stepping into the gap left by the disappearance of the Achaean thalassocracy; in Syria a number of Aramaean kingdoms made their appearance with their capitals at Damascus, Hama, Aleppo, Carchemish, Sindjirli, Milid and other places. In Palestine the Israelites established the two kingdoms of Israel and Judah; in Transjordan the Kingdoms of Ammon, Moab and Edom came to being. Furthermore, the Aegeans introduced the use of iron for weapons and tools, and thus gave birth to a new culture, the Iron Age which replaced the culture of the Bronze Age. The pottery prevalent in Palestine and Phoenicia during the Iron Age is well represented in the Museum in Cases 9 and 10. The contrast between the two is great; whereas the Phoenician ceramic industry shows strong Aegean influence, (Figs. 10-13) that of Syria and Palestine betrays a remarkable decline in form to that of the preceding pottery of the Late Bronze Age.

The Israelites evinced a tendency to break curves into angles (Fig. 14) and paid no attention to their pottery. The demand for vessels was great and in order to cope with it, vessels became utilitarian and were mass produced without heed to grace of form or careful finish. Similarly, the Aramaeans of the hinterland were ready to copy the ideas of their neighbours but they had no eye for graceful forms or beauty of finish. Indeed a small juglet made of black or red ware in Israel had a very long lease of life. It was first made sometime in the Twelfth Century but it continued in production, with some minor changes in the length of the neck and the position of the handle, until well into the Seventh Century. The reason for this discrepancy between the two cultures, is not far to seek; whereas the coast was settled by Aegeans who came with a ready made culture of a high order, the hinterland was settled by nomads who came from the desert, and had to spend sometime schooling themselves in the culture of their subjects before they were able to become civilized. Thus the Israelites in some cases actually started making some pots by hand, when the Phoenicians were already producing beautifully decorated graceful forms.

The hybrid character of the civilizations of Syria, Phoenicia and Palestine, is best reflected in the large number of seals made in the area in imitation of foreign seals. Some of the Syro-Hittite and other local seals of the period may be seen in the bronze table-case between Cases 9 and 10. Scaraboids were copied from Egyptian examples, and cylinder seals from Assyrian examples. The presence of the latter reflects the rise of Assyrian power in the Near East during the Ninth Century BC. and the eventual destruction of some of the kingdoms that arose after the Twelfth Century, such as the Aramaean Kingdoms of Syria and the Kingdom of Israel.

The short-lived Neo-Babylonian or Chaldaean Empire which succeeded the Assyrian left little impression on the Mediterranean seabord. However the succeeding Persian Empire witnessed great changes in culture. Because of the far flung dominions of the "King of Kings", as the Persian monarch was called, closer contact was established between the Greek and the Asiatic world because of the Greek colonies that were established on the West Coast of Asia Minor. Thus side by side with the local pottery, (Fig. 15) which differed only in minor details from the pottery of the earlier period, Corinthian and Attic black-figured vases start making their appearance in the Near East in increasing numbers. The Persian Period also witnessed the introduction of coinage in the Near East. In addition to the gold and silver darics minted in Susa and Persepolis, there were special issues for the Fifth satrapy or province which comprised Phoenicia, Syria and Palestine. The tolerance of the Persian rulers was such that many autonomous cities like Aradus, Tyre and Sidon were allowed to mint their own coins. Contact with the Greek world not only brought exquisite articles of Greek manufacture into the Near East, but it also gave rise to schools of sculpture which copied the techniques of the Greeks in stone and terra cotta. Many examples of Phoenician sculpture and terra cotta figurines which betray strong Greek influence are exhibited in Case 11 of the Museum, while many specimen of Greek, Persian and Phoenician coins of the period may be seen in the special coin case between Cases 10 and 11.

Cases 12-14 represent the University's share of Cypriote pottery which was presented by Cesnola and which formed the core around which the Museum grew, as well as many other pots of Cypriote origin purchased by private collectors and eventually acquired by the University. This collection is of great importance for drawing parallels and differences between the early Cypriote pottery and the pottery of corresponding ages in Palestine, Phoenicia, Syria, Iraq and Egypt.

In the iron-bound-case, Case C, there is displayed the small collection of inscribed tablets which were acquired by the University in Mesopotamia or in Asia Minor. Among them is a Cappadocian tablet left behind by the Assyrian trading community which was settled outside Kanesh (modern Kultepe) in the Twentieth and Nineteenth Centuries BC.

The Museum has in the past acquired some objects which were actually found in Greece and Egypt, and which belong to the 7th and 5th Centuries BC. Most of these were collected by the late Rouvier, and the University bought the bulk of his collection as stated previously. They are at present exhibited in Sections A and B of Case 15, close to the collection of artefacts of contemporary date found in Phoenicia, Syria and Palestine and exhibited in Case 11. The objects are of great importance for a comparative study of the culture of the Near East in relation to the neighbouring countries.

The conquest of the Near East by Alexander the Great during the last third of the Fourth Century BC., and the consequent rise of the great Hellenistic Kingdoms of the Ptolemies and the Seleucids is reflected in the large assortment of Hellenistic artefacts in Case 15, Section C and Case 18 Section A-D. Purely Greek forms replace to a large extent the Oriental types of pottery that prevailed previously, and even when the latter persisted, they are strongly influenced by the new Greek types (Figs. 16 & 17).

In the Coin Case previously referred to there is a representative selection of Ptolemaic and Seleucid coins, which were minted or were current in the area, while the coins of autonomous cities such as Tyre, Sidon, Berytus, Aradus and others who had acquired political autonomy during the last chaotic years of the Seleucid Kingdom echo the disruption and decentralization which eventually brought that kingdom to an end.

In Case 18 Sections E and F, an attempt was made to show the struggle between Rome and Parthia in the First Century BC. over the Near East. Pottery of the Herodian Period is placed close to the glazed pottery of Parthian origin.

Pottery, bronze objects and sculpture of the Roman Period occupy the remaining sections of Case 18; they are a tribute to the might of Rome and her position as final arbiter in the destiny of the Near East. Other objects of the Roman Period are exhibited in a number of other cases. The coin case contains a selection of Roman Republican and Imperial coins, while the large selection of autonomous city coins bears witness to the tolerance of Roman rule, and the respect that Rome held for the culture of the Near East, from which she learnt a great deal, and which she undertook to diffuse in the semi-civilized provinces of Gaul, Britain, Germany and Spain. In Case 17, a selection of lamps of the period is included. In Case 19 there is a large collection of blown glass vases of the Near East (Figs 19 & 20); blown glass, like moulded translucent glass, was an invention of the Phoenicians. Roman figurines in bronze (Figs 21 & 22), Roman toilet articles in bronze and bone, Roman jewellery in gold, silver, bone and ivory, and Roman musical instruments in bone can be seen in Cases 16 and 24, and in the bronze case between Cases 15 and 18.

A special case, Case 21, which is internally lit, shows an array of beautiful Roman intaglios or cut gems in carnelian, agate and other semi-precious stones. The Roman era saw the rise of Christianity and the eventual triumph of the new faith after a period of intense persecution. From the First Century AD., a small number of articles of Christian manufacture started making their appearance, and proceeded to increase with the propagation of the new faith. A number of heresies arose before the Council of Nicaea finally formulated the articles of Christian dogma and belief. The Gnostic heresy was very strong at one time, as the various Gnostic seals exhibited in Case 24 testify. However all Christians wore the small cross in silver or bronze as an amulet, hence the relatively large number of crosses in the same case, which also contains objects used in the Christian sacrament such as silver spoons with bone handles for the wine, and silver picks for the bread.

The Roman era saw the penetration of Roman civilization into the Syrian Desert. In the period of anarchy of the Third Century, the formerly insign-ificant caravan city of Palmyra managed under its great queen Zenobia to expand into a great metropolis and become the seat of an Arab Empire stretching from the Sea of Marmora in the North to Nubia in the South, embracing all Phoenicia, Palestine, Egypt and Syria as far as the Euphrates. The heart of the Empire was Palmyra which was the seat of a peculiar culture influenced alike by Persian and Roman cultures but retaining an individuality and a character entirely its own. The Palmyrenes had their peculiar mythology and beliefs, their system of writing their architecture and their art. Examples of sculptured Palmyrene busts are to be seen in the alcove at the southeast corner of the Museum (Fig. 23). Palmyrene art had a special appeal to the later Arabs, who when they arrived in the Seventh Century AD., chose Palmyrene sculpture for their model in preference to Sassanian or Byzantine models.

With the Edict of Milan in AD. 312, the Christians came to profess their faith openly, and their numbers multiplied. They proceeded to decorate their lamps with crosses and with representations of their places of worship, as the selection of lamps of the period in Case 17 testifies.

The move of the capital from Rome to Constantinople in AD. 330 eventually converted the Roman Empire into an Oriental state. Mass production of pottery left little place for good taste and refinement, except at the Imperial Court or in the palaces of the rich. There was a marked decline in execution in almost every type of production. Pottery declined in form and decoration, coinage degenerated and became utilitarian at the expense of fine execution in design and technique. When the Arabs came and lopped off large sections of the Byzantine Empire and annihilated the Sassanian Persian Empire, the decline was arrested. The Arabs, not possessing a culture of their own, and at the outset looking with disdain on both the Byzantine and Sassanian cultures as effeminate, eventually created a new virile culture combining the virtues of both. They started schools of ceramic art which combined the graceful Hellenistic forms and the blue glaze of the Parthians and produced something quite unique. The glazed technique of the Arabs was later copied and developed first by the Persians and later by the Seljuks, but the art has never died, and glazed tile factories still flourish in Damascus, Jerusalem and Baghdad. Examples of Early Arab, Persian and Seljuk glazed pottery and tiles can be seen in Case 22, while examples of the later glazed ware of Damascus are exhibited in the adjoining case, Case 23.

In addition to the various artefacts exhibited in the Museum, the University has recently received a generous gift from the French Archaeological Mission to Iran in the form of a large collection of pottery from the Mission's excavations at Susa dating from the Fourth Millennium BC. to the Ninth Century AD. At present this collection is exhibited in an annex to the Museum, but eventually it will be exhibited with the rest of the collection. This valuable addition to the Museum will be of great help in the comparative study of the ceramic industry of the various parts of the Near East.

Besides the numerous objects on display in the Museum, the University has a large selection of objects stored in a special room for the benefit of the students. These objects are within easy reach and can be examined closely. By coming to know the articles used by the people of the past intimately, the students become better acquainted with the people themselves, who thus become real people and not just hazy phantoms of bygone days, elusive of perception.

Historians are no prophets; but, to use the words of the late Petrie, on reviewing the past they cannot but dimly forecast the future progress of mankind; they are thus favoured with a very long lease of life, adding millennia to their age by their study of the past, and projecting their lives into a hazy, but by no means uncertain future.

1. Juglet of Copper Age from Byblos.
2. Small jar of the Copper Age from Palestine.
3. Painted piriform juglet of the Middle Bronze Age from Syria.
4. Trumpet based bowl of the Middle Bronze Age from Palestine.

5. Bronze toggle pins of the Middle and Late Bronze Ages from Phoenicia.
6 & 7. Bronze figurine of Reshef from the Late Bronze Age from Phoenicia.

8. Decanter of the Late Bronze Age from Phoenicia.
9. Mycenaean stirrup vase of the Late Bronze Age from Phoenicia.
10. Beer jug of the Early Iron Age with strainer spout from Phoenicia.
11. Beer jug of the Iron Age from Phoenicia.

12. Painted juglet of the Iron Age from Phoenicia.
13. Small juglet of the Iron Age from Phoenicia.
14. Decanter of the Middle Iron Age from Palestine.
15. Slender jar of the Persian Period from Phoenicia.

16. Hellenistic storage jar from Phoenicia.
17. Hellenistic jar from Phoenicia.
18. Moulded glass bowl of the Iron Age from Phoenicia.
19. Glass bowl of the Roman Period from Phoenicia.

20. Glass vase of the Roman Period from Phoenicia.
21. Terra cotta figurine of the Roman Period from Phoenicia.
22. Bronze figurine of Venus of the Roman Period from Phoenicia.
23. Palmyrene bust of the Third Century AD.